WORKBOOK:

ATLAS OF THE HEART

(An Essential Guide to Mapping Meaningful Connection and the Language of Human Experience).

1

DEDICATION

To You, My Reader

This is an EIGHT (8) STEP GUIDE TO SUSTAINING MEANINGFUL CONNECTIONS.

INSTRUCTIONS

1. HAVE A PEN/PENCIL WITH YOU AS YOU STUDY THIS WORKBOOK
2. IN THE "NOTES" SECTION, WRITE DOWN THE THOUGHTS THAT RAN THROUGH YOUR HEAD WHILE NAVIGATING EACH STEP
3. PRACTICE ALL YOU LEARN FROM THIS WORKBOOK.

NAME:

_____

_____

AGE:

_____

OCCUPATION:

_____

_____

_____

RELATIONSHIP STATUS:

_____

_____

The heart is the pathway to the soul.

To gain access to the soul of another, one must carefully navigate through the hurdles along the way.

Each connection, each emotion can either lead you closer to the soul or take you farther away.

As a map leads you right so will the steps in this book.

Learn them and you will be granted access to the beauty that is the soul of another.

STEP 1

"HAVE MEANINGFUL CONVERSATIONS"

Communication is the live wire of every relationship.

One of the best ways to gain access to a person is by asking good questions on important issues pertaining to the person.

This indicates interest.

"One who asks questions never misses his path".

TASK

Ask questions on dreams, goals, passion, dislikes, interests, etc.

TIPS

In other not to make the person feel ambushed, start up the conversation on a light note, share some personal experiences then ask about theirs.

(if you are not in a very close relationship with the person, avoid questions that are too personal).

NOTES

_____

_____

_____

_____

_____

_____

_____

_____

_____

_____

_____

_____

_____

_____

_____

_____

_____

_____

STEP 2

"COMMITMENT AND CONSISTENCY"

Nothing beats consistency.

Be consistent and committed in strengthening the connection.

TASK

Think of ways to strengthen the bond or connection you have with someone.

Write them down.

Go ahead and do exactly what you've written down.

TIPS

Be creative. Start with the little things you can do and gradually grow your list.

<u>NOTES</u>

_____

_____

_____

_____

_____

_____

_____

_____

_____

_____

_____

_____

_____

_____

_____

_____

_____

_____

<u>STEP 3</u>

"FACE TIME OVER TEXT TIME"

This basically means meeting in person rather than depending on social media alone.

Connections are mostly strengthened when people spend time often in person.

TASK

Plan hangout sessions and set up meeting dates.

TIPS

Select a place that is liked by both of you and go there.

It is easier to create time for a hang out when it is in a place of interest.

NOTES

<u>STEP 4</u>

"SHOW APPRECIATION"

Constantly show that you appreciate the person's company.

Rather than complain about what the person isn't doing, show gratitude for what is being done.

TASK

Write a letter to the person, stating all the things you are grateful for.

TIPS

Be very elaborate and specific. Do not be generally thankful. Rather, mention each reason one after the other.

<u>NOTES</u>

STEP 5

"OPENNESS AND VULNERABILITY"

Meaningful connections are made and sustained by being open and through the display of vulnerability.

This builds trust and increases value.

TASK

Open up about a matter to the
person.

TIPS

Speak your truth. Do not try to
hide anything.

NOTES

<u>STEP 6</u>

"ACTIONS OVER WORDS"

Words are soothing but actions justify and give quality to words.

To gain access and keep a connection with a person, your actions towards that person must speak louder than your words.

TASK

Do something to show how valuable that person is to you.

TIPS

It doesn't have to be too grand but make sure your intentions are well displayed.

NOTES

STEP 7

"BE UNDERSTANDING"

To have a meaningful and lasting connection with someone, you must understand their flaws, pattern of displaying emotions, personality, amongst other things.

TASK

Observe how the person displays emotion and acts in a certain way.

Ask questions about it.

TIPS

You can only truly understand a person when you have answers to the things that causes confusions or misunderstandings.

When asking these questions, do not pester.

NOTES

_____
_____
_____
_____
_____
_____
_____
_____
_____
_____
_____
_____
_____
_____
_____
_____
_____
_____
_____

STEP 8

"LOVE UNCONDITIONALLY"

Show love and care regardless of the barriers, distance, weaknesses, flaws, and so on.

Unconditional love remains the greatest tool for gaining access to a person.

TASK

Make up your mind to love unconditionally and do just that.

TIPS

Be genuine in displaying unconditional love.

Do not fake it or do it for selfish gains.

NOTES

WE HAVE SUCCESSFULLY COME TO THE END OF THIS WORKBOOK.

AFTER FOLLOWING THE ABOVE STATED STEPS, EVALUATE THE QUALITY OF YOUR CONNECTIONS AND KEEP REPEATING THESE STEPS!

HOW HAS THIS WORKBOOK HELPED YOU?

PERSONAL NOTES

OTHER THINGS

Made in the USA
Monee, IL
22 December 2021